OUR HOLY FAITH

OUR HOLY FAITH

BOOK ONE

GOOD SHEPHERD

TAN Books
Gastonia, North Carolina

Originally published in 1964 as Our Holy Faith Book I: My Father and Mother on Earth and in Heaven by Bruce Publishing Company and reprinted in 1998 by The Neumann Press.

Nihil Obstat:
John A. Schulien, S.T.D.
Censor Librorum
Imprimatur:
William E. Cousins
Archbishop of Milwaukee
April 9, 1964

This TAN Books edition has been re-typeset and enhanced with additional content and revisions, including modernized language and updates to the practices of the Catholic Church. Catechism questions and answers have been replaced with the TAN edition of The Third Council of Baltimore: Baltimore Catechism 1–4.

Scripture quotes are adapted from the Douay-Rheims 1899 American Edition.

Content revisions and updates by Elisa Torres
Interior design by Caroline Green
Interior illustrations by Jordan Avery
Cover design by www.davidferrisdesign.com

ISBN: 978-1-5051-1920-6

Published in the United States by
TAN Books
PO Box 269
Gastonia, NC 28053
www.TANBooks.com
Printed in the United States of America

Contents

Publisher's Note

The original editions of the *Our Holy Faith* series textbooks were published between 1959 and 1964. They were compiled by many different authors over the course of several years. Consequently, the texts varied in their organization from year to year, with similar sections appearing with different names throughout the series and often in varying sequences.

For greater ease of use and consistency, we have reorganized each book so that the Catechism lessons, tests, and other exercises are placed at the end of each relevant chapter or lesson. We have also included answer keys for your convenience in the back of each book.

While the teachings in the original editions remain relevant due to the enduring truths of our Faith, it was necessary to update other aspects in order to more accurately reflect the Church today. These new editions have been revised to incorporate some of the changes to the practices of the Catholic Church.

To the extent possible, we have adapted the text to reflect both the ordinary and extraordinary forms of the Mass and liturgical calendars. In addition to these updates, we have inserted, where relevant to the text, traditional prayers and quotes from the Bible, the Catechism, and the saints.

This new Our Holy Faith series is faithful to the work of the original authors. It honors the fundamental and unchanging truths of the Catholic Church and is heavily influenced by tradition. We believe it is the catechesis you can trust with your children's faith.

To the Students

Dear Boys and Girls,

This is your first religion book. It will tell you many things about God and your Catholic Faith.

Your teacher will read the stories to you until you learn how to read. But you can study the pictures. Every picture tells you a wonderful story.

When you learn about God you will love Him more and more. Then, someday you will be happy with Him in heaven.

God Bless You,
The Publisher

CHAPTER 1

The Church—God's House

We Go to Church

What We Do In Church

We dip our fingers in holy water.
We bless ourselves.

We genuflect.
We adore Jesus.

We pray.

We walk out quietly.

Why do we do this in church?

Jesus and the Little Children

Long, long ago Jesus said,
"Let the little children come to me."
Jesus blesses the children.
Jesus loves the children.
Children love Jesus, too.

We Visit Jesus in Church

Now, too, Jesus says,

> "Let the little children
> come to me."
> Jesus, we know You
> are here.
> Jesus, we love You.
> Jesus, bless us, too.

O Jesus, the Friend of
little children,
bless the little children
of the whole world.

Jesus Comes at Mass

Offertory

The priest offers bread.
Soon it will be the Body
of Jesus.

He offers wine.
Soon it will be the Blood
of Jesus.

Consecration

"This is My Body."
Jesus, You are here.
"This is My Blood."
Jesus, You are here.

Holy Communion

Jesus loves us.
Jesus comes to us.

The Priest—God's Special Helper

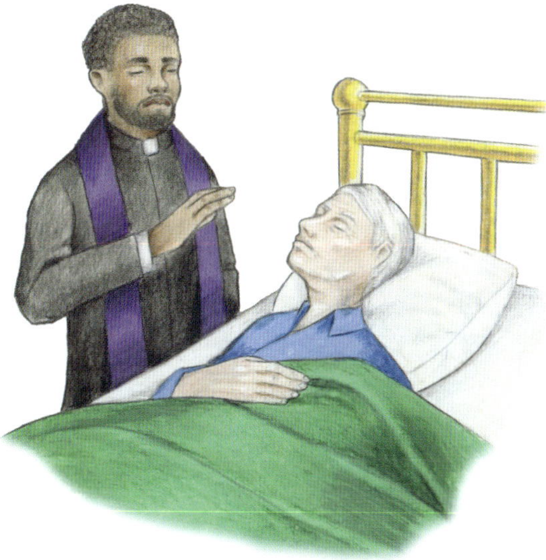

The priest helps us to love God.

He helps us on the way to heaven.

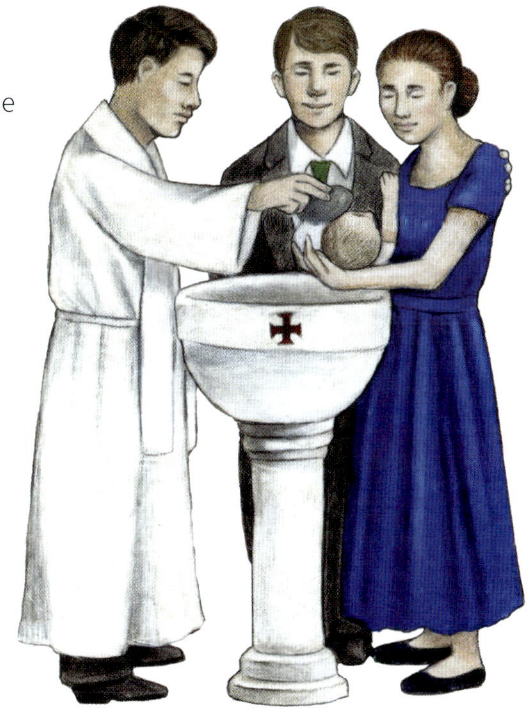

Can you tell other ways the priest helps us?

Do you know your parish priests?

Things We Can See in the Church

Altar

Crucifix

Tabernacle

Sanctuary Light

Candles

Statue

Missal

Communion Rail

Can you name all these objects? Can you find them in the picture?

The Sign of the Cross

I belong to God.
I make God's special sign.
I make the Sign of the Cross.
Can you tell when?

In the name of the Father	and of the Son	and of the Holy	Spirit.	Amen.

CHAPTER 2

God Our Heavenly Father

God Loves Us

God is our heavenly Father.
God loves us.
He takes care of us.
God shows us His love in many ways.
Can you tell how?

On My Way To Heaven . . .

God made me.
I belong to God.
God wants me to be happy with Him in heaven.

God Sees Me

What does God see?
God is everywhere.
God can see everything.
But we cannot see God.
God is a Spirit.

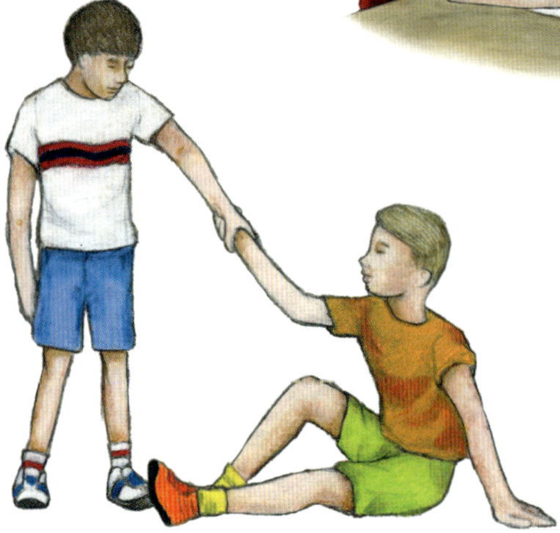

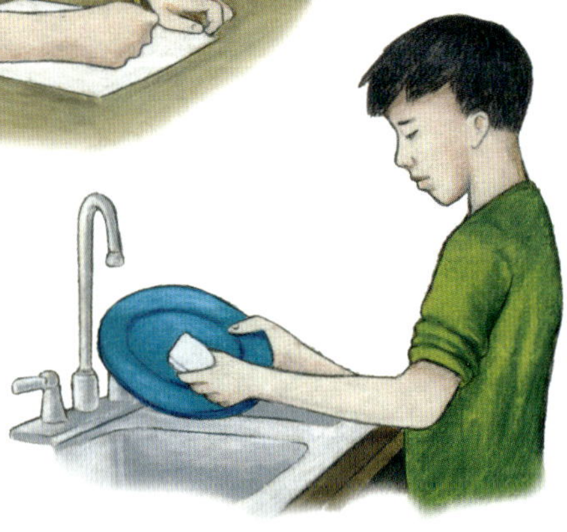

God Hears Me

What can God hear at home?

What can God hear in church?

What can God hear at play?

What can God hear at school?

God can hear everything.
God can hear me at all times.

God Lives In Me

I am a child of God.
When I was baptized God came to live in me.
My soul was made holy.
My soul was made pleasing to God.

The Blessed Trinity

There is only one God.
There are three Persons in God:
the Father,
the Son,
the Holy Spirit.
We call the three Persons in God the Blessed Trinity.

God Created the Angels

God made the angels to praise Him.

The good angels went to heaven.

The bad angels were punished.

My Angel And I

Angel of God, my guardian dear,
To whom His love entrusts me here,
Ever this day be at my side,
To light and guard, to rule and guide.
Amen.

God the Creator

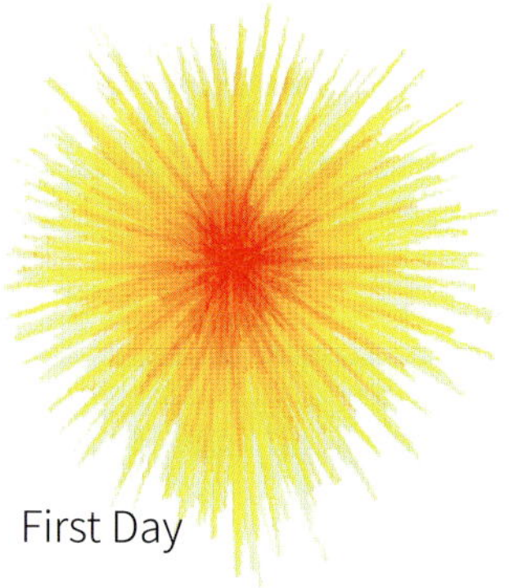

First Day

Second Day

Third Day

Fourth Day

Fifth Day

Sixth Day

God made all things.
God is the Creator of heaven and earth.

Our First Parents

God created Adam.
God created Eve.
God gave Adam and Eve His grace.
They were very happy.
Adam and Eve are our first parents.
God placed them in a Garden of Paradise

The Fall of Adam and Eve

Adam and Eve are not happy.
They did not obey God.
They lost God's grace.
But God will send a Savior to save Adam and Eve.
The Savior will save all people.

CHAPTER 3

The Lord's Prayer

Jesus, Friend of little children,
Teach us how to pray.
You were once a little Boy,
Tell us what to say.

Prayer Is Talking to God

I can tell Him many things.

Jesus, I adore You.

Jesus, I'm sorry.

Thank You, Jesus.

Jesus, please help me.

What other things can you tell Jesus?

All for the Love of God

Dear God, I love You.
I will pray for love of You.
I will work for love of You.
I will play for love of You.
My whole day will be a loving prayer.

Pray

Work

Play

The Lord's Prayer—The Best Prayer

"Our Father who art in heaven"

I call on my heavenly Father.
He is everywhere, but He is in heaven in a special way.

"hallowed be Thy name"

Hallowed means holy.
God's name is holy.
I tell God I want His name praised.

"Thy kingdom come"

I want everyone to know and love God.
I will spread the Good News of the Gospel.

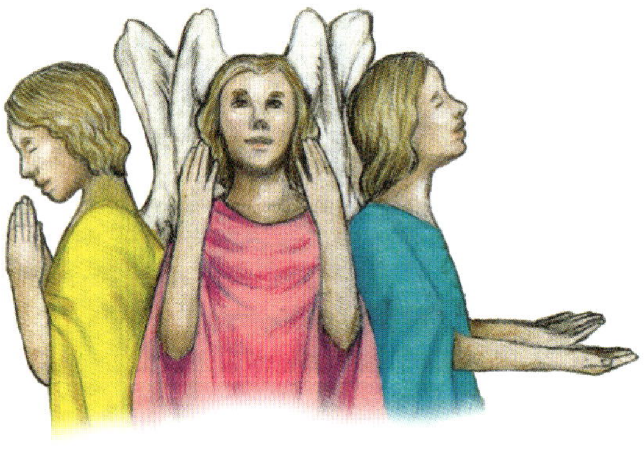

"Thy will be done on earth as it is in heaven"

Angels and saints do God's will in heaven.
I will do God's will, too.
I will work and play with love.

"Give us this day our daily bread"

We ask God for all our needs.
We ask God for food for our body and soul.

"and forgive us our trespasses as we forgive those who trespass against us"

God forgives us when we are sorry.
God wants us to forgive others, too.

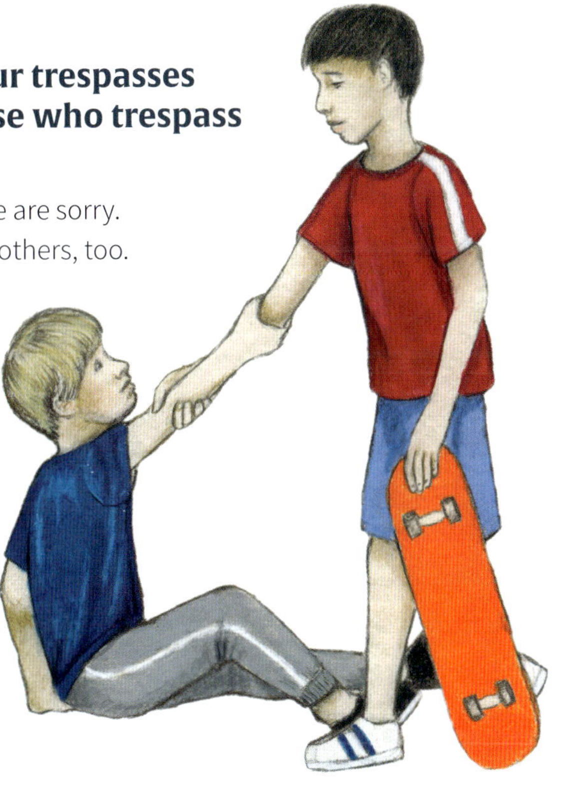

"and lead us not into temptation"

The bad angels want me to do wrong.
I will ask God to help me do right.

"but deliver us from evil. Amen."

I ask God to keep me safe
from all harm every day.

CHAPTER 4

God's Goodness in Sending His Son to Us

Waiting for the Savior

God promised to send a Savior.
The good people waited and waited.
They prayed and prayed.
They wanted the Savior to come.

We Too Are Waiting for the Savior to Come

We get ready for the coming of Jesus.

Come, Lord Jesus,
Come from heaven;
All the world is waiting for Thee.
Son of God and Son of Mary,
Low we bow our heads before Thee.[1]

Pray

Work

Obey

Can you tell other ways we can get ready?

1 Sr. Cecilia, S.C., *We Sing and Play* (Ginn, 1957), p. 41.

Mary Was Waiting for the Savior Too

God sent an angel to Mary.
Angel Gabriel said, "Hail, full of grace, the Lord is with thee."
God wants her to be the Mother of Jesus.
Mary will do what God wants.

The Hail Mary

We Praise and Honor Mary

"Hail Mary"

I greet Mary the way Angel Gabriel did.

"full of grace! the Lord is with Thee"

Mary is free from all sin.
Mary is pleasing to God.

"Blessed art thou among women"

Mary visited Elizabeth.
Elizabeth said these words to Mary.
Mary praised God.

"and blessed is the fruit of thy womb, Jesus."

Jesus is the Son of Mary.
Jesus is holy, too.
Jesus is God.

We Ask Mary to Help Us

"Holy Mary, Mother of God"

I know Mary is the Mother of Jesus.
I want Mary to ask Jesus to help me.

"pray for us sinners, now"

I want Mary to help me now.

"and at the hour of our death."

I ask Mary to help me when I die.

Baby Jesus Comes

Mary and Joseph went to Bethlehem.
There was no room in the inn.
So they went to a stable.
Soon Baby Jesus came.
The angels sang and sang.
Jesus is our Savior.
Christmas is the birthday of Jesus.

An angel told the shepherds the good news.
The shepherds came to visit Jesus.
They loved Jesus.
Jesus was happy to see them.

Three Wise Men came to visit Jesus.
They offered Him gifts.
Jesus was happy to see them.
Jesus blessed the Wise Men.

CHAPTER 5

The Childhood of Jesus

The Holy Family Goes to Egypt

An angel told Joseph to
hurry away.
He told Joseph to hurry
away with Mary and
Jesus.
Jesus was in danger.
Joseph and Mary
went at once.
They went far away
to Egypt.

The Holy Family in Nazareth

Jesus, Mary, and Joseph came back from Egypt.
They came to live in Nazareth.
Jesus, Mary, and Joseph are the Holy Family.
They had a poor home.
But it was a happy home.

Joseph the Head of the Family

Joseph is the head of the Holy Family.
Joseph is the foster father of Jesus.
Joseph served Mary and Jesus.

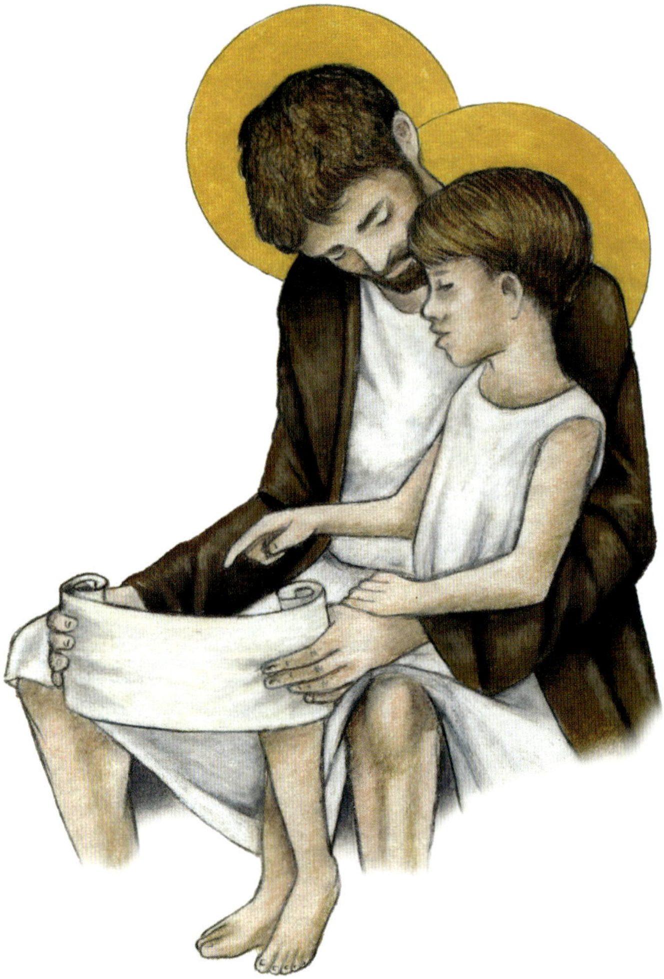

Mary the Mother of the Holy Family

Mary is the Mother of Jesus.
Mary loved her family.
Mary served Jesus and Joseph.

Jesus Teaches Me What to Do

Jesus showed us what to do.
Jesus did all things well.
I will try to do all things well like Jesus.

Jesus prayed.

I will pray.

Jesus helped.

I will help

Jesus worked.

I will work.

Jesus was kind.

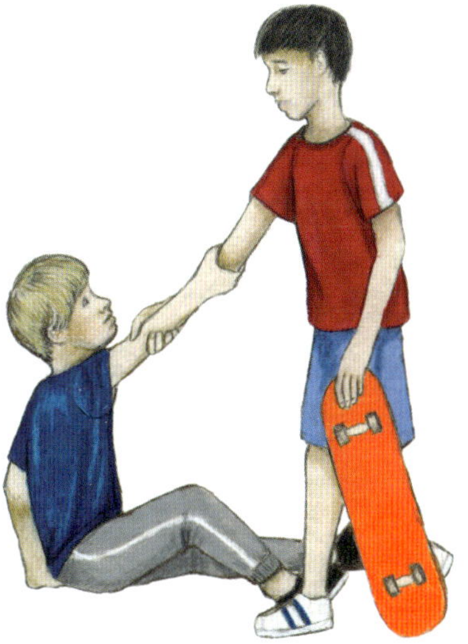

I will be kind.

When Jesus Was Twelve Years Old

Jesus went with Mary and Joseph to the temple.
They went to the temple to pray.
Soon it was time to go home.
But Jesus did not go home with Mary and Joseph.
Mary and Joseph could not find Jesus.
After three days they found Him in the temple.
Jesus taught others about God, His heavenly Father.

CHAPTER 6

The Public Life of Our Lord

Jesus Is Baptized

Jesus was baptized by his cousin John.
God the Holy Spirit came upon Jesus.
God the Father spoke from heaven.
"This is my beloved Son, in whom I am well pleased," He said.
Jesus is the Son of God.

Jesus and His Helpers

It was time for Jesus to begin His work.
He chose twelve men to help Him.
These men went with Jesus.
They became Jesus' Apostles.

Jesus is teaching His friends.
He is teaching them about God.
He is teaching them how to pray.

Jesus Thinks of Others

Jesus went to a wedding feast.
The people needed help.
Mary asked Jesus to help them.
He changed water into wine.

Many people came to hear Jesus.
They stayed a long time.
Soon they were hungry.
Jesus blessed five loaves of
bread and two fishes.
Then there was food for all.

Jesus Shows His Power

Jesus and the Apostles were in a boat.
Soon a big storm came up.
The Apostles were afraid.
But Jesus said, "Peace, be still."
At once the storm stopped.

The Apostles were far out at sea.
They saw someone walking on the water.
It was Jesus.
He can walk on water.
Jesus is God.

Jesus Raises the Dead to Life

A little girl was dead.
Jesus held her hand and said, "Girl, arise."
The girl lived again.

Lazarus was dead
and buried.
Jesus said,
"Lazarus, come
forth!"
The dead man
came out.
He was living
again.

Jesus Makes the Sick Well

A blind man said, "Jesus,
help me.
Let me see."
Jesus was kind.
He made the
blind man see.

Ten sick men cried,
"Jesus, have pity on us."
Jesus made them all well.
But only one man thanked Jesus.

CHAPTER 7

The Greatest Proof of Jesus' Love—the Passion and Death

Jesus Loves Us

We adore Thee, O Christ, and we bless Thee; because by Thy holy cross Thou has redeemed the world.

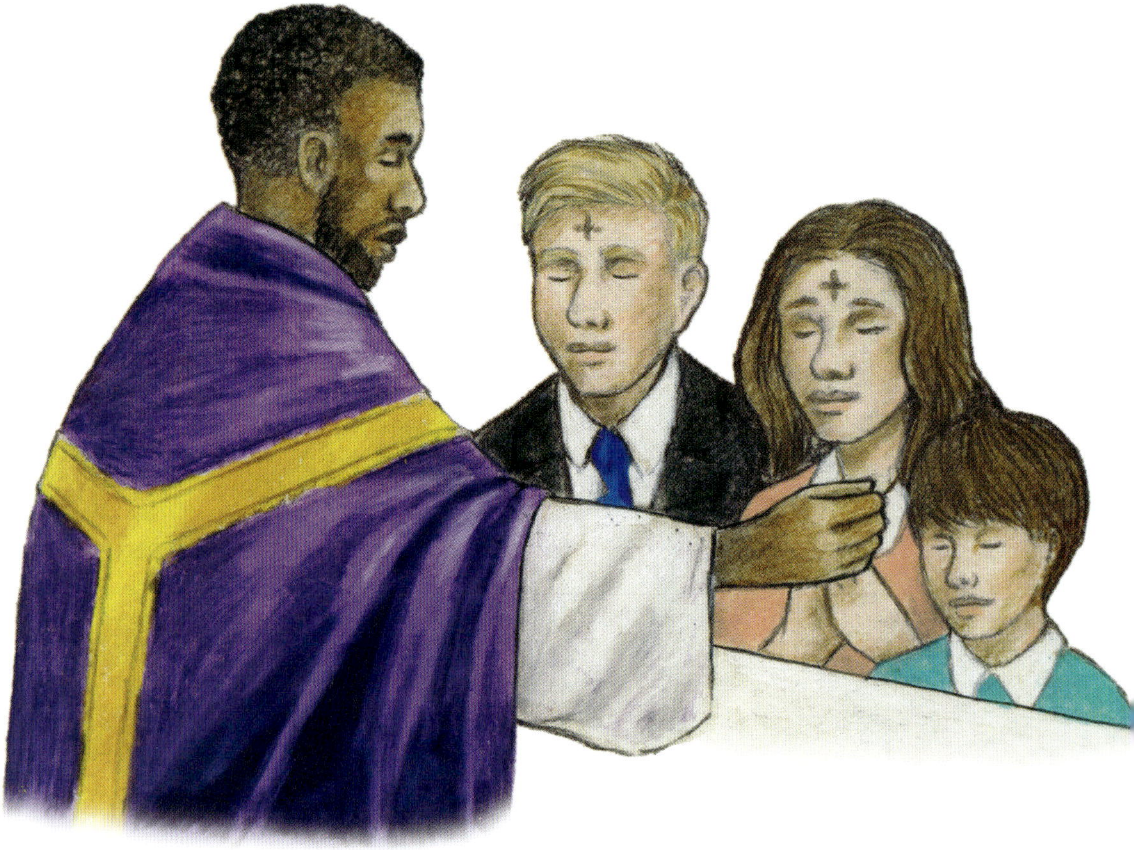

Lent—A Time of Love

Lent is a special time to show Jesus our love.
The priest puts a cross on my brow with blessed ashes.
The cross helps me to think of Jesus.
I think of Jesus in a special way.

Something Special for Jesus During Lent

Jesus, we love You.

Palm Sunday Long Ago

The people loved Jesus.
"Hosanna, to the Son of David,"
they sang.
But they did not know that
Jesus was God.

Palm Sunday Now

We show Jesus our love.
Jesus is our King.
Jesus is God.

Holy Thursday Long Ago

Jesus had His last supper with the Apostles.
He took bread and blessed it.
The bread became the Body of Jesus.
Jesus took wine and blessed it.
The wine became the Blood of Jesus.
Then Jesus gave Himself to the Apostles.

Holy Thursday Now

We visit Jesus in church.
We thank Him for giving
Himself to us.

The Priest and Jesus

The priest is another Christ.
At Mass he does what Jesus did.
He says what Jesus said.

Jesus said the first Mass.
The priest says Mass every day.
"This is My Body," the priest says.
The bread becomes Jesus' Body.

"This is My Blood," the priest says.
The wine becomes Jesus' Blood.
We receive Jesus in Holy Communion

Jesus Suffered to Make Up for Our Sins

Jesus is sad.

Jesus is silent.

Jesus is scourged.

Jesus is crowned with thorns.

The Way of the Cross

Jesus carried a heavy Cross.
How it did hurt Him!
As He went along, He fell three times.
Jesus met His Mother on the way.
She was very sad.
Some people were kind to Jesus.
At last Jesus reached the top of Mount Calvary.

By His Holy Cross Jesus Redeemed the World

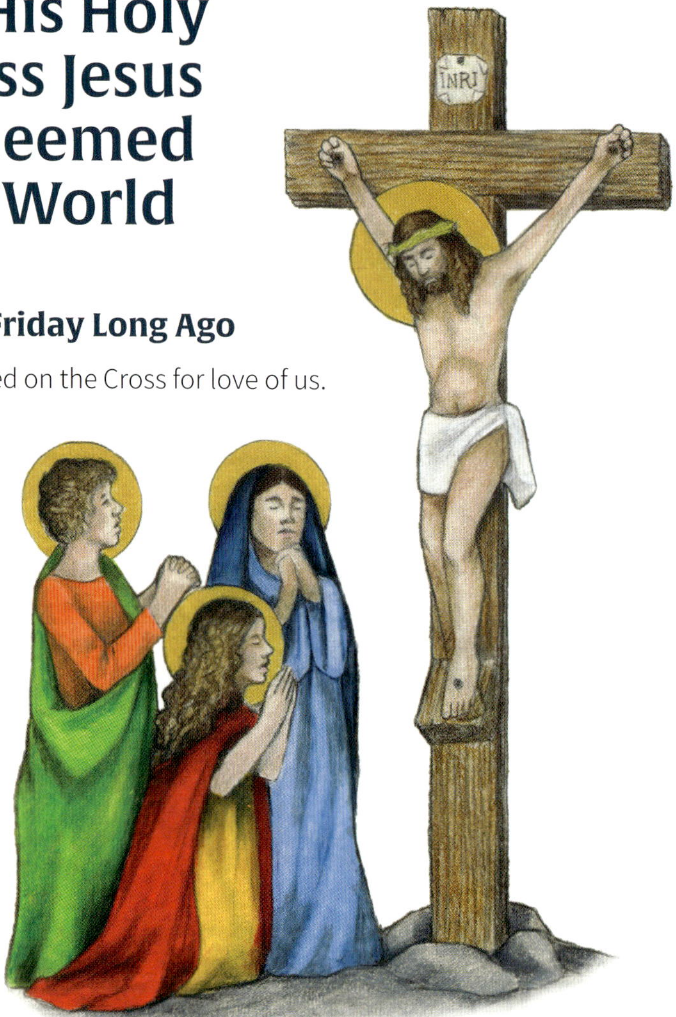

Good Friday Long Ago

Jesus died on the Cross for love of us.

Good Friday Now

We thank Jesus for dying for us.
We kiss the Cross to show our love.

Jesus Is Buried

Kind people took Jesus' body off the Cross.
They took care of Jesus' body.
They carried the holy body to a grave.

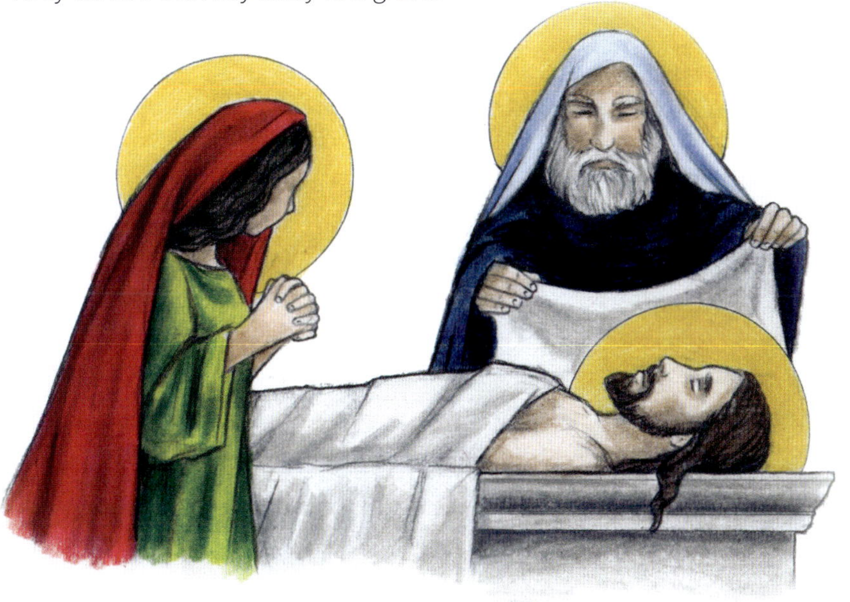

Jesus was buried.
The tomb was closed.
Guards kept watch.

Jesus Visits His Friends

When Jesus died on the Cross, His soul went down to limbo.
Jesus told His friends good news.
Soon they will be happy with Jesus in heaven.

CHAPTER 8

The Resurrection and Ascension

Jesus Rose from the Dead

On Easter Sunday Jesus came back to life.
He rose from the dead by His own power.
His body was most beautiful; it was glorified.
Jesus proved He is truly God.

Jesus Made His Friends Happy

Jesus came to His Mother.

Mother Mary was happy to see her Son living again.

The Apostles believe Jesus rose from the dead.
Now they know that Jesus is truly God.

Jesus Gave Us an Easter Gift

On Easter day Jesus came to His Apostles.
"Peace be to you," He said.
He gave them the power to forgive sin.
This is His Easter gift to us.
Jesus came to His friends again.
This time He spoke to Thomas.
"My Lord and my God," Thomas said.
Now Thomas believes Jesus rose
from the dead.
Before he did not.

Jesus Surprised His Friends

Jesus walked with His friends.
They did not know it was Jesus.

Jesus took bread and blessed it.
Then they knew it was Jesus.
They believed He rose from the dead.

The Apostles and Jesus

The Apostles worked all night.
They did not catch any fish.
A Man said, "Cast the net to the right of the boat."
They caught many fish.
Then the Apostles knew the man was Jesus.
Jesus was kind to Peter.
He said, "Feed My lambs; feed My sheep."
Jesus made Peter the first Pope.

Jesus Goes to Heaven

Once again Jesus spoke to His friends.
"Go and teach all nations," He said.
Jesus promised to send the Holy Spirit to help them.
Then Jesus blessed His friends.
Soon He was gone.
He went to His Father in heaven; body and soul.

Our Resurrection

Someday, we will rise from the dead.
Our body and soul will come together again.
Then we will be happy forever with God in heaven.

CHAPTER 9

God the Father and God the Son Show Their Love by Sending God the Holy Spirit

Come, Holy Spirit, Creator blest,
And in our hearts take up Thy rest;
Come with Thy grace and heavenly aid,
To fill the hearts which Thou hast made.

I Believe In the Holy Spirit

The Holy Spirit is God.
He is the third Person of the Blessed Trinity.
The Holy Spirit gives me sanctifying grace.
Grace makes my soul holy.
The Holy Spirit helps me live God's life.

Glory be to the Father, and to the Son, and to the Holy Spirit. As it was in the beginning, is now, and ever shall be, world without end. Amen.

The Holy Spirit Comes

The Holy Spirit came as Jesus had promised.
He came on the tenth day after Jesus went back to heaven.
The Bible tells us,
"There appeared to them parted tongues as of fire."
The Apostles were all filled with the Holy Spirit.

The Holy Spirit Helps

The Holy Spirit made the Apostles brave.
He helped them speak to the people.
The Holy Spirit helped the Apostles teach the people about God.
He helped the Apostles teach the people about the Catholic Church.
On this day the Holy Spirit made the Church known to the world.

"Go and Teach All Nations"

The Apostles did as Jesus told them to do.
They went out to teach the people about God.
God the Holy Spirit helped them in their work.

The Catholic Church

The Church is God's family on earth.
The Pope is the head of the Church.
The bishops and priests are his helpers.
We, too, belong to God's family.

The Catholic Church as a Loving Mother

The Catholic Church is our loving Mother.
She helps us to live God's life.
She gives us the sacraments.
The sacraments keep us close to Jesus.

CHAPTER 10

Mary, Our Heavenly Mother

Mary, We Love You

Dear Mother Mary
In heaven above,
Look down on your children
And teach us to love.
Teach us to love you
And your Son, Jesus, too;
Then, someday, dear Mother
We'll be in heaven with you.

Mary Is Taken Into Heaven

Jesus wanted Mary to be with Him.
Mary was taken into heaven, body and soul.
This is called Mary's Assumption.
From heaven Mary watches over us.
She is our heavenly Mother.

Jesus Honors His Mother

Jesus wanted to show Mary His love for her.
He wanted to honor her in a special way.
Jesus crowned Mary as Queen of heaven and earth.
Mary is the Queen of the angels and of the saints.
Mary is our Queen and our Mother, too.
We honor Mary upon earth.
We show her our love, too.

We Show Mary Our Love

The rosary is Mary's favorite prayer.
Mary wants us to say the rosary often.
When we say the rosary, we show Mary that we love her.
Mary promised great blessings to those who say the rosary every day.
We know how to say the prayers on the rosary.

Mary Protects the Church

Mary wants all the people to know God.
She wants all the people to love God.
She wants all the people to serve God.
Mary helps the Church in her work for God.

We Go to Jesus Through Mary

Jesus came to us through Mary.
We go to Jesus through Mary.
Jesus is the King of the Universe.
Jesus, I crown you King of my heart.

Prayers

The Sign of the Cross

In the name of the Father, and of the Son, and of the Holy Spirit. Amen.

The Glory Be

Glory be to the Father, and to the Son, and to the Holy Spirit. As it was in the beginning, is now, and ever shall be, world without end. Amen.

The Lord's Prayer

Our Father who art in heaven,
Hallowed be Thy name;
Thy kingdom come;
Thy will be done on earth as it is in heaven.
Give us this day our daily bread;
And forgive us our trespasses as we forgive those who trespass against us;
And lead us not into temptation,
But deliver us from evil. Amen.

The Hail Mary

Hail Mary, full of grace! the Lord is with thee; blessed art thou among women, and blessed is the fruit of thy womb, Jesus. Holy Mary, Mother of God, pray for us sinners, now and at the hour of our death. Amen.

The Apostles' Creed

I believe in God, the Father almighty, Creator of heaven and earth, and in Jesus Christ, His only Son, Our Lord, who was conceived by the Holy Spirit, born of the Virgin Mary, suffered under Pontius Pilate, was crucified, died and was buried; He descended into hell; on the third day He rose again from the dead; He ascended into heaven, and is seated at the right hand of God the Father almighty; from there He will come to judge the living and the dead. I believe in the Holy Spirit, the holy Catholic Church, the communion of saints, the forgiveness of sins, the resurrection of the body, and life everlasting. Amen.

An Act of Faith

O my God, I believe all the truths which the Holy Catholic Church teaches, because Thou hast made them known.

An Act of Hope

O my God, because Thou art all-powerful, merciful, and faithful to Thy promises, I hope to be happy with Thee in heaven.

An Act of Love

O my God, because Thou art all-good, I love Thee with my whole heart and soul.

An Act of Contrition

O my God, I am heartily sorry for having offended Thee, and I detest all my sins, because of Thy just punishments, but most of all because they offend Thee, my God, Who are all-good and deserving of all my love. I firmly resolve, with the help of Thy grace, to sin no more and to avoid the near occasions of sin. Amen.

Prayer to the Guardian Angel

Angel of God, my guardian dear, to whom His love entrusts me here, ever this day be at my side, to light and guard, to rule and guide. Amen.

The Blessing Before Meals

Bless us, O Lord, and these Thy gifts which we are about to receive from Thy bounty, through Christ Our Lord. Amen.

Grace After Meals

We give Thee thanks for all Thy benefits, O Almighty God, who livest and reignest forever. Amen.
May the souls of the faithful departed, through the mercy of God, rest in peace. Amen.

Morning Offering

O Jesus, through the Immaculate Heart of Mary, I offer Thee my prayers, works, joys, and sufferings of this day for all the intentions of Thy Sacred Heart, in union with the Holy Sacrifice of the Mass throughout the world, in reparation for my sins, for the intentions of all our relatives and friends, and in particular for the intentions of the Holy Father. Amen.

First Communion Catechism

The starred Catechism questions serve as a basis for evaluating student progress in the knowledge and understanding of the doctrinal truths presented within the units.

Lesson 1: The Purpose of Man's Existence

***1. Who made you?**
God made me.

***2. Did God make all things?**
Yes, God made all things.

***3. Why did God make you?**
God made me to show His goodness and to make me happy with Him in heaven.

***4. What must you do to be happy with God in heaven?**
To be happy with God in heaven I must know Him, love Him, and serve Him in this world.

Lesson 2: God and His Perfections

***5. Where is God?**
God is everywhere.

***6. Does God know all things?**
Yes, God knows all things.

***7. Can God do all things?**
Yes, God can do all things.

***8. Did God have a beginning?**
No, God had no beginning; He always was.

***9. Will God always be?**
Yes, God will always be.

Lesson 3: The Unity and Trinity of God

***10. Is there only one God?**
Yes, there is only one God.

***11. How many Persons are there in God?**
In God there are three Persons—the Father, the Son, and the Holy Spirit.

***12. What do we call the three Persons in one God?**
We call the three Persons in one God the Blessed Trinity.

***13. How do we know that there are three Persons in one God?**
We know that there are three Persons in one God because we have God's word for it.

Lesson 4: The Incarnation

***14. Did one of the Persons of the Blessed Trinity become man?**
Yes, the Second Person, the Son of God, became man.

***15. What is the name of the Son of God made man?**
The name of the Son of God made man is Jesus Christ.

***16. When was Jesus born?**
Jesus was born on the first Christmas Day, more than two thousand years ago.

***17. Who is the Mother of Jesus?**
The Mother of Jesus is the Blessed Virgin Mary.

***18. Is Jesus Christ both God and man?**
Yes, Jesus Christ is both God and man.

Lesson 5: The Redemption; the Church

***19. Why did God the Son become man?**
God the Son became man to satisfy for the sins of all men and to help everybody to gain heaven.

***20. How did Jesus satisfy for the sins of all men?**
Jesus satisfied for the sins of all men by His sufferings and death on the cross.

***21. How does Jesus help all men to gain heaven?**
Jesus helps all men to gain heaven through the Catholic Church.

Lesson 6: Sin; Original Sin

***22. What is sin?**
Sin is disobedience to God's laws.

***23. Who committed the first sin?**
The bad angels committed the first sin.

***24. Who committed the first sin on earth?**
Our first parents, Adam and Eve, committed the first sin on earth.

***25. Is this sin passed on to us from Adam?**
Yes, this sin is passed on to us from Adam.

***26. What is this sin in us called?**
This sin in us is called original sin.

***27. Was anyone ever free from original sin?**
The Blessed Virgin Mary was free from original sin.

Lesson 7: Actual Sin

28. Is original sin the only kind of sin?
No, there is another kind of sin, called actual sin.

29. What is actual sin?
Actual sin is any sin which we ourselves commit.

30. How many kinds of actual sin are there?
There are two kinds of actual sin: mortal sin and venial sin.

31. What is mortal sin?
Mortal sin is a deadly sin.

32. What does mortal sin do to us?
Mortal sin makes us enemies of God and robs our souls of His grace.

33. What happens to those who die in mortal sin?
Those who die in mortal sin are punished forever in the fire of hell.

34. What is venial sin?
Venial sin is a lesser sin.

35. Does venial sin make us enemies of God or rob our souls of His grace?
No, venial sin does not make us enemies of God or rob our souls of His grace.

36. Does venial sin displease God?
Yes, venial sin does displease God.

Lesson 8: The Sacraments; Baptism, Confirmation

*** 37. How does the Catholic Church help us to gain heaven?**
The Catholic Church helps us to gain heaven especially through the sacraments.

***38. What is a sacrament?**
A sacrament is an outward sign, instituted by Christ to give grace.

*** 39. What does grace do to the soul?**
Grace makes the soul holy and pleasing to God.

***40. What sacraments have you received?**
I have received the sacrament of Baptism.

***41. What did Baptism do for you?**
Baptism washed away original sin from my soul and made it rich in the grace of God.

42. Are you preparing to receive other sacraments?
I am preparing to receive the sacraments of Confirmation, Penance and Reconciliation, and Holy Eucharist.

43. What will Confirmation do for you?
Confirmation, through the coming of the Holy Spirit, will make me a soldier of Jesus Christ.

Lesson 9: Penance and Reconciliation

44. What is the sacrament of Penance and Reconciliation?
Penance and Reconciliation is the sacrament by which sins committed after Baptism are forgiven.

45. What must you do to receive the sacrament of Penance and Reconciliation worthily?
To receive the sacrament of Penance and Reconciliation worthily I must:

1. Find out my sins.
2. Be sorry for my sins.
3. Make up my mind not to sin again.
4. Tell my sins to the priest.
5. Do the penance the priest gives me.

Lesson 10: How to Make a Good Confession

46. How do you make your confession?
I make my confession in this way:

1. I go into the confessional and kneel.
2. I make the sign of the cross and say: "Bless me, Father, for I have sinned."
3. I say: "This is my first confession" (or, "It has been one week, or one month, since my last confession").
4. I confess my sins.
5. I listen to what the priest tells me.
6. I say the act of contrition loud enough for the priest to hear me.

47. What do you do after leaving the confessional?
After leaving the confessional, I say the penance the priest has given me and thank God for forgiving my sins.

Lesson 11: The Holy Eucharist

48. What is the sacrament of the Holy Eucharist?
The Holy Eucharist is the sacrament of the body and blood of Our Lord Jesus Christ.

49. When does Jesus Christ become present in the Holy Eucharist?
Jesus Christ becomes present in the Holy Eucharist during the Sacrifice of the Mass.

50. Do you receive Jesus Christ in the sacrament of the Holy Eucharist?
I do receive Jesus Christ in the sacrament of the Holy Eucharist when I receive Holy Communion.

51. Do you see Jesus Christ in the Holy Eucharist?
No, I do not see Jesus Christ in the Holy Eucharist because He is hidden under the appearances of bread and wine.

52. What must you do to receive Holy Communion?
To receive Holy Communion I must:

1. Have my soul free from mortal sin.
2. Not eat or drink anything for one hour before Holy Communion. But water may be taken at any time before Holy Communion.

53. What should you do before Holy Communion?
Before Holy Communion I should:

1. Think of Jesus.
2. Say the prayers I have learned.
3. Ask Jesus to come to me.

54. What should you do after Holy Communion?
After Holy Communion I should:

1. Thank Jesus for coming to me.
2. Tell Him how much I love Him.
3. Ask Him to help me.
4. Pray for others.